B is for Bluenose

A Nova Scotia Alphabet

Written and Illustrated by Susan Tooke

Acknowledgments:

A special thanks for Wally Hayes; my editor, Aimee Jackson; and to Richard Rudnicki for his constant support.

I would like to thank the following people and organizations for their help in making this exploration of Nova Scotia possible:

Mary MacKinnon and Nova Scotia Tourism, Culture and Heritage; Cole Hayes; James and Diana Hazelton; The Cape Breton Miner's Museum; Andrew Hebda; Nova Scotia Museum of Natural History; Parks Canada; Wayne Kerr, Alan, Evan and Andy Syliboy; Carrie-Ann Smith and Pier 21's Scotiabank Research Centre; Jenna Boone, Donald Agnew, Deborah Skilliter, Rhonda Kelly and The Joggins Fossil Institute; Parks Canada/Alexander Graham Bell National Historic Site of Canada; Kathleen Martin and the Canadian Sea Turtle Network; Peggy and Shimon Walt; Maral Perk; Cantor Ari Isenberg; Mimisu and Lala Lee; Patrice Boulianne (Blou); Jill Barber; Dutch Robinson; Novelee Buchan; Trevor Gould; Anthony Rissesco; the Halifax Herald Limited; Nova Scotia Power; Ron Robinson and the Pugwash Park Commission; Barb Robson, "Old Nova Scotian Quilts" by Scott Robson & Sharon MacDonald (Halifax: Nimbus Publishing and the Nova Scotia Museum, 1995); Hazel Poole and "Copper"; Zoe Lucas; Rev. Alfreda Smith and Kalum Willis; Dr. Henry Bishop and The Black Cultural Centre for Nova Scotia; the photographic reference for "V" by William Ivor Castle, Canada Department of National Defence / Library and Archives Canada / PA- 022744; Catherine Cottreau-Robins; Kevin Robins and the Army Museum, Halifax Citadel; Lisa Wolfe, Barry Hiltz, Wade Corkum and the Ross Farm Museum; Derek Fenton; Ellen Kenchington and Kevin MacIsaac, Fisheries and Oceans Canada, Bedford Institute of Oceanography; Tamara Gates-Hollingsworth, Chris Fogarty and Environment Canada; Lou McNally; Robyn Bremner, DRUM! Live Inc.

*For Richard Rudnicki, my husband,
and for Nova Scotia, our home, with love.*

SUSAN

Sleeping Bear Press™

310 North Main Street, Suite 300
Chelsea, MI 48118
www.sleepingbearpress.com

© 2008 Sleeping Bear Press is an imprint of Gale, a part of Cengage Learning.

Printed and bound in Canada.

First Edition

10 9 8 7 6 5 4 3 2 1

Library of Congress Cataloging-in-Publication Data

Tooke, Susan.
B is for bluenose: a Nova Scotia alphabet / written and illustrated by Susan Tooke.
p. cm.
Summary: "This illustrated alphabet book includes history, landscapes, sea creatures, provincial symbols, and more. From A to Z simple poems introduce topics such as Cape Breton, eelgrass, Joggins, osprey, and Vimy Ridge. Detailed expository text provides more information on each topic for more experienced readers"—Provided by publisher.
ISBN 978-1-58536-362-9
1. Nova Scotia—Juvenile literature. 2. Alphabet books—Juvenile literature. I. Title.
F1037.4.T66 2008
971.6—dc22   2008012616

Welcome to Nova Scotia, Canada's ocean playground! The province of Nova Scotia is diverse in landscape and ancient in heritage.

The Peggy's Point Lighthouse, featured on the cover, is perhaps the most photographed lighthouse in Canada. It is a popular destination for travellers. Scenic Peggy's Cove is still a working fishing village.

Come explore the vibrant culture, the beauty of our rugged land, and the rich history that make up our unique province.

> "I have travelled around the globe. I have seen the Canadian and American Rockies, the Andes, the Alps and the Highlands of Scotland, but for simple beauty Cape Breton outrivals them all."
> —Alexander Graham Bell

Aa

The Annapolis Valley is located in the western part of the Nova Scotia peninsula. The North and South Mountains protect the valley from harsh weather. This shelter from the mountains creates a mild climate perfect for growing vegetable and fruit crops.

The first record of an apple crop in Canada was in 1610, harvested by Acadian settlers in the Annapolis Valley. Today there are more than 1,000 farms in the valley, where not only apples are grown, but also grapes, strawberries, blueberries, pumpkins, potatoes, and many other vegetables. The fertile valley is often referred to as the breadbasket of Nova Scotia because of the many crops that are grown here.

The valley has become famous for its delicious apples. The town of Kentville celebrates the arrival of spring with the Apple Blossom Festival. Harvest festivals in autumn include the Annapolis Valley Pumpkin Festival with pumpkin carving, pumpkin people, and giant pumpkin weigh-offs where pumpkins can weigh as much as a moose!

A is for Annapolis Valley

Springtime's full of scented blossoms,
in the orchards pink and white.
Pick rosy apples in the autumn;
reach up high, then take a bite.

The skirl (high-pitched wail) of the bagpipes is often heard in Nova Scotia (Latin for "New Scotland"). Scottish people began immigrating to Nova Scotia in the early 1600s. While living in Scotland under British rule, the Scottish people were forbidden to speak their Gaelic language, and were not permitted to wear the tartans of their clans. The playing of the bagpipes was also outlawed. In Nova Scotia, the Scots were free to live as they chose.

Festivals such as the Gathering of the Clans and the Highland Games celebrate Scottish history and culture. Today, Scots form the largest cultural group in Nova Scotia and the bagpipes can be heard across the province.

Bb

B is for Bagpipes

Lines of pipers march in drills.
Music echoes through the hills.
Parades of plaids go marching by,
while Celtic tunes soar to the sky.

Picturesque Cape Breton Island is well known for its rugged beauty and its world famous Cabot Trail. This scenic highway winds around the island's northern shore. The island is separated from the mainland of Nova Scotia by the Strait of Canso, but is connected by a man-made rocky causeway (the deepest causeway in the world!) so that cars and even trains can go between the island and the mainland. In the centre of the island is Brad d'Or Lake, where the water is both salty from the sea and fresh from the rivers that empty into it. Bald Eagles live and fish along the rocky shorelines. Cape Breton Highlands National Park, located at the northern part of the island, is a protected wilderness of mountain forests, river valleys, and ocean shores. The vast highlands mark the highest elevation in the Atlantic region, and are an extension of the Appalachian mountain chain. Humpback whales can be seen in the waters offshore.

C is for Cape Breton

Surrounded by the North Atlantic,
Cape Islanders upon the sea.
Miners dug beneath the ocean
in the deep dark collieries.

Because of its rich coastline and waters, both fishing and coal mining rose up as industries in Nova Scotia. The Mi'kmaq were the first fishermen off the cape. Later settlers began fishing for cod off the waters off Cape Breton, then called Île Royale. Today, along with a variety of marine species, the Atlantic Snow Crab is an important part of the fisherman's livelihood. Boats called Cape Islanders have been used in Nova Scotia for more than a hundred years. These boats are known for their durability in often rough and unstable waters.

Because of the specific geological makeup of the area, Nova Scotia is rich with coal. The first commercial coal mine opened in Cape Breton in 1720 and mining continued here for 280 years! The pits could stretch for kilometres out under the Atlantic Ocean, hundreds of metres below sea level. In the early years, child miners, some less than ten years old, worked in the collieries (coal mines) with their brothers and fathers. Miners faced dangers of methane gas explosions, bumps when the floor of the pit would rise up, and rock falls when the roof would collapse.

The early Acadians were French colonists who settled in what was then called *Acadie* (Acadia), and is now the Canadian Maritimes. In the 1630s the first dykes (dikes) were built at Port-Royal. These earthen mounds blocked the tides from flooding the land. This enabled the settlers to farm the reclaimed salt marsh and its fertile soil.

The clever *aboiteau*, a wooden pipe with a wooden flap inside, was placed at the base of the dyke. The aboiteau allowed the rainwater to drain off the land, while preventing the tides from surging back in. Within several years, rains removed the salt from the soil and it was perfect for planting.

Spreading out to the lands surrounding the Midas Basin, the Acadians continued to build dykes, controlling the flow of rivers and streams. This process prevented the Bay of Fundy tides, the highest in the world, from flooding the reclaimed marsh.

Today you can still see evidence of the dykes in the rich farmland surrounding Grand-Pré National Historic Site.

D is for Dykes

Acadian farms and fields now stand
along the banks of Fundy's shores.
Dykes block seawater from the land,
so farmers can plant on the moors.

Ee

Long ribbons of green grasses wave gently in the quiet ocean waters near the shore. Eelgrass is a flowering plant, not seaweed. Eelgrass can form thick, underwater forests in estuaries, the places where rivers and oceans meet. These forests are important nurseries for many species of fish, including the American eel. These eels live in fresh-water rivers and lakes, but return to the sea to spawn (lay eggs) in an area southwest of Bermuda. After the eel larvae hatch, they make the year-long journey back to the Maritimes. Hiding in the eelgrass stems, these transparent "glass eels," mature into green elvers, a perfect disguise in these underwater forests. Eels can live more than 50 years! Other species that live in the eelgrass are the pipefish, the threespine stickle-back, periwinkles, and sand dollars.

Eelgrass is also important because it helps to prevent erosion of the seabeds. It is an important food source for ducks, Canada Geese, and Brants. These water-fowl feed on the seeds, roots, and leaves.

E is for Eelgrass

Eelgrass ribbons wave in bays.
Ducks and geese on eelgrass graze.
Sea life grows between the blades,
and moves along when summer fades.

F is for Fortress

Look back in time at two nations' proud forts,
where the French and the British guard rival ports.
Louisbourg and The Citadel facing the sea,
along the coastline lives our history.

A fortress, or fortification, is a permanent military post built to defend cities and harbours. It can include several structures or buildings. During the 1700s and 1800s, many countries were fighting for land. The Louisbourg and Citadel fortresses were built by France and Great Britain to protect their land claims.

In 1713 the French settled Louisbourg on the east coast of Île Royale (Cape Breton Island). It became a prosperous port, thriving on the rich cod fishery of the Grand Banks. Louisbourg was attacked several times by the British during this period of struggle. At the Fortress of Louisbourg National Historic Site, you can go back in time to the year 1744 and see what the life of the townsfolk was like.

The Citadel overlooks present day Halifax much as it did when completed in 1856. It was built to protect this vital British naval port against land strikes from the United States. Today it is a National Historic Site where visitors can participate in life as it was in 1869. Don't be startled with the firing of the noon canon! It is a traditional marking of time in Halifax.

Ff

G is for Glooscap (Klooscap)

Into the rock so long ago,
symbols were carved where waters flow
of Mi'kmaq spirits and cultures vast;
from elder down to child they're passed.

The Mi'kmaq have lived for thousands of years in what is now known as the Maritime Provinces. In Mi'kmaq spiritual belief, the Creator made the world, with all its plants, birds, and animals. Then the Creator caused lightning to strike the sand and the spiritual being Glooscap was created. Glooscap, this gigantic, superhuman being, is the centre of many creation stories that have been passed down through generations.

Mi'kmaw artist Alan Syliboy finds inspiration for his work in the Mi'kmaq petroglyphs (rock drawings) found in the ancient rock of Nova Scotia. Alan's pride in his heritage and his interest in Mi'kmaq spiritualism are evident in his art—a celebration of family and culture he shares with his son and grandson, pictured with him in the illustration. Notable Mi'kmaq include poet Rita Joe, activist Anna Mae Aquash, hockey player Chad Denny, and fiddler Lee Cremo.

H is for Harbour

Travellers sail over the sea.
Foghorns blow mournfully.
Tugboats guide ships to dock,
while in the harbour sailboats rock.

Called *Chebucto* (Great Harbour) by the Mi'kmaq, Halifax Harbour is one of the world's largest and deepest natural harbours, reaching inland for a distance of 28 kilometres! In this huge, ice-free inlet of the ocean, ships are protected from the open seas of the North Atlantic.

Halifax Harbour is the largest port in Atlantic Canada. The capital district of Halifax Regional Municipality (HRM) includes Halifax, Dartmouth, Bedford, and Sackville. Halifax and Dartmouth sit on either side of the harbour, connected by the A. Murray MacKay and Angus L. MacDonald suspension bridges.

Beneath the MacKay Bridge on the Halifax end is Seaview Park, built on the site of historic Africville. During the 1960s this community was destroyed and its 400 black residents relocated to make room for the bridge. Today former residents gather each July to honour the spirit of their community.

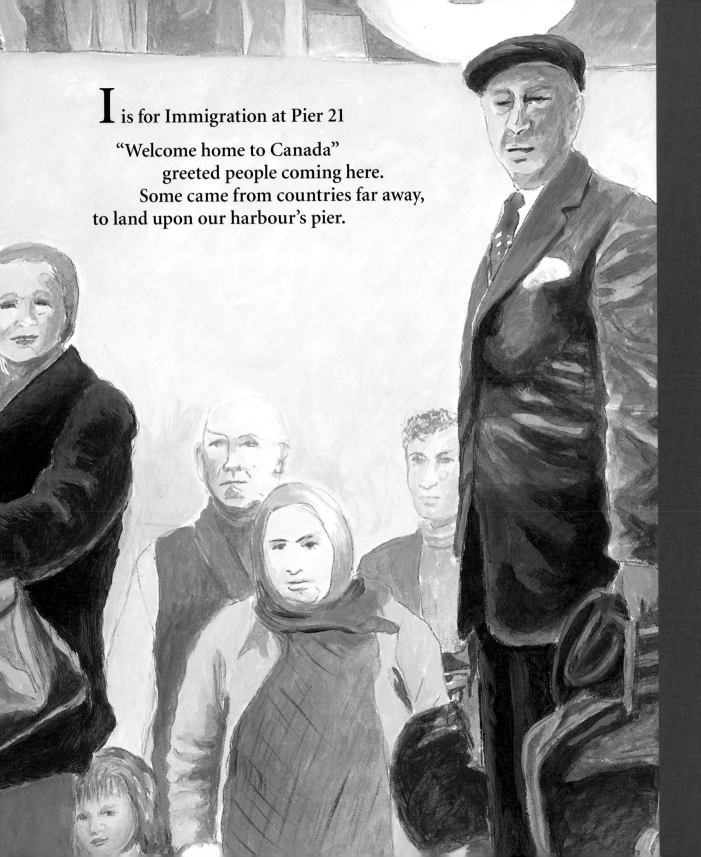

I is for Immigration at Pier 21

"Welcome home to Canada"
greeted people coming here.
Some came from countries far away,
to land upon our harbour's pier.

Pier 21 is located in Halifax Harbour. The pier, now a National Historic Site, celebrated its seventy-fifth birthday in 2003. This was the entry point to Canada for more than one million immigrants. During World War II, Pier 21 was used as a staging area for troops leaving for and returning from Europe.

Immigrants came mainly from European countries. Some came to find work. Some came to escape their own war-torn countries. Many were children who were evacuated from European countries to escape the devastation of war. And many thousands of immigrants were the brides and children of Canadian soldiers who had married while they were in Europe.

In later years more immigrants began arriving by air instead of sea, so Pier 21 officially closed to immigration in March of 1971. It reopened in 1999 as Canada's Immigration Museum, celebrating the Pier's historical significance to Canada's cultural diversity. Selected as one of the Seven Wonders of Canada, you can visit Pier 21 today and experience what it was like to read "Welcome Home to Canada," leaving one homeland for a new one.

Joggins is a community in Nova Scotia where the Joggins Fossil Cliffs are found. The towering cliffs are located in an inlet at the northernmost part of the Bay of Fundy. Today scientists recognize the Joggins Fossil Cliffs as one of the most important sites in the world for studying life during the Carboniferous Period (the "Coal Age").

Fossils are the preserved remains of animals and plants—such as a skeleton, leaf, or footprint—embedded in rock. The powerful tides from the Bay of Fundy have caused the cliffs to erode over time, revealing fossilized remains of life forms within the rocks. At Joggins, reptile fossils have even been found buried inside petrified 300-million-year-old tree trunks, 100 million years before dinosaurs!

The illustration shows us what some of the creatures from this ancient time might have looked like. Imagine a time when early lizards scampered over the forest floor and giant dragonflies hovered overhead!

The Joggins Fossil Cliffs were designated a UNESCO World Natural Heritage Site in 2008.

Jj

J is for Joggins

Tides wash stone from cliffs of red.
Creatures crept from the seabed.
Seabirds cry along the shore,
while Joggins's fossils we explore.

K is for Kite

Bell had dreams to sail and soar,
while flying kites over Brad d'Or.
Eyes look up with hopes to fly,
like graceful birds across the sky.

Best known for inventing the telephone, Alexander Graham Bell was also interested in aeronautics at a time when many thought it impossible that people would ever fly. Born in Scotland in 1847, he later moved to Nova Scotia after a visit to Cape Breton Island, where he lived until his death in 1922.

At his home in Baddeck, he conducted experiments in flight using kites. Bell tried many designs, but the tetrahedron, a four-sided kite made up of equilateral triangles, was the most successful. It provided strength and stability without added weight. In 1905 a kite made of 1,300 tetrahedrons, named the Frost King, lifted a man into the air, proving that the kite could lift more than its own weight. Two years later the Cygnet, a kite with over 3,000 tetrahedrons, was towed behind a steamship, carrying a man 51 metres into the air.

Because of its efficiency in design, Bell's tetrahedral shape led to advances in architecture and bridge design.

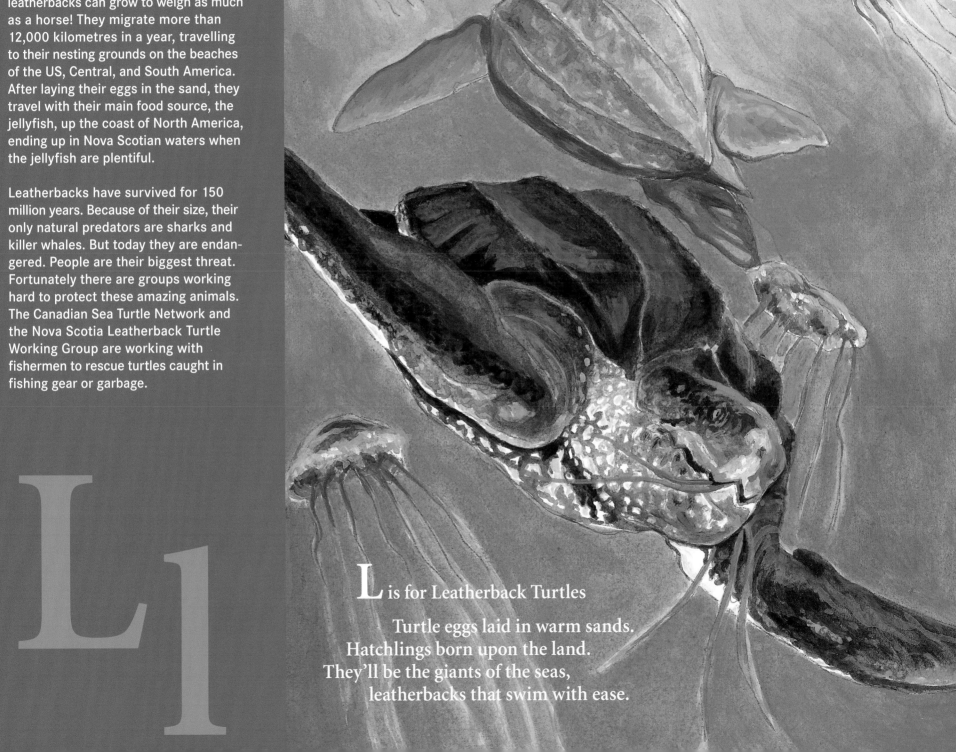

Leatherbacks are the largest turtles in the world. As hatchlings, they are small enough to fit in a child's hand, but adult leatherbacks can grow to weigh as much as a horse! They migrate more than 12,000 kilometres in a year, travelling to their nesting grounds on the beaches of the US, Central, and South America. After laying their eggs in the sand, they travel with their main food source, the jellyfish, up the coast of North America, ending up in Nova Scotian waters when the jellyfish are plentiful.

Leatherbacks have survived for 150 million years. Because of their size, their only natural predators are sharks and killer whales. But today they are endangered. People are their biggest threat. Fortunately there are groups working hard to protect these amazing animals. The Canadian Sea Turtle Network and the Nova Scotia Leatherback Turtle Working Group are working with fishermen to rescue turtles caught in fishing gear or garbage.

L1

L is for Leatherback Turtles

Turtle eggs laid in warm sands.
Hatchlings born upon the land.
They'll be the giants of the seas,
    leatherbacks that swim with ease.

M is for Music

A festival with Celtic tunes!
Jazz bands rock 'neath summer moons.
Drum beats Mi'kmaq, and Acadian,
guitar, fiddle, and accordion.

Music festivals abound in Nova Scotia. The Scotia Festival of Music, The Stan Rogers Festival, and The Atlantic Jazz Festival, are just a few. Acadian music, with its fiddle, step dance, and accordion, and Mi'kmaq chants, songs, and drumming, echo across the province keeping our traditional music alive.

The Cape Breton Celtic influence is felt in the music of Sarah McLachlan, Mary Jane Lamond, and Natalie MacMaster. The country/folk sound is heard in the popular music of Rita MacNeil. One of the biggest international stars to come out of our province is Anne Murray, born in Springhill. She has won countless music awards. Hank Snow (1914-1999) born in Brooklyn, Nova Scotia, was a Hall of Fame country music singer and songwriter and recorded over 100 albums. Portia White (1911-1968), born in Truro, was a classical singer who achieved international fame.

From hip-hop music to Symphony Nova Scotia, music is in the heart of every one of us!

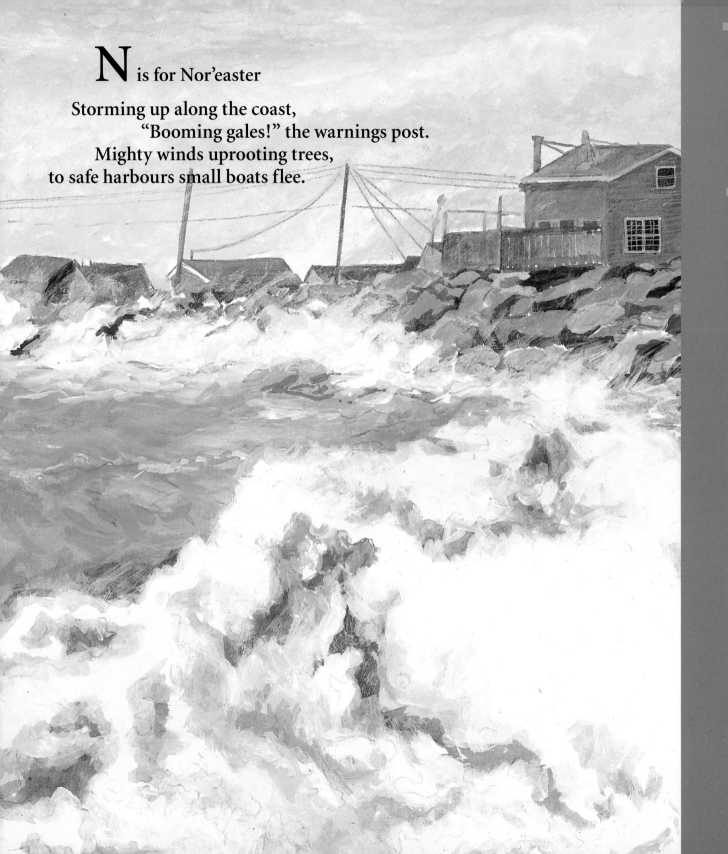

N is for Nor'easter

Storming up along the coast,
"Booming gales!" the warnings post.
Mighty winds uprooting trees,
to safe harbours small boats flee.

Gale force winds, heavy rain, blizzards, and pounding surf are the typical results from a nor'easter. They move in a counterclockwise rotation with the driving winds coming from the northeast. Nor'easters are most common in Atlantic Canada in fall and winter, and can rival hurricanes with the amount of damage caused. Trees are brought down, power lines are broken, rivers overflow their banks, and beaches suffer from erosion.

One of the worst nor'easters was the Saxby Gale of 1869. When the gale struck, winds reached hurricane force and the tide rushed up the Bay of Fundy, flooding all of the communities along the shores. In the August Gales of 1926 and 1927, six Lunenburg Schooners were lost off Sable Island, along with more than one hundred brave fishermen. Another well-known nor'easter was the Halloween Nor'easter of 1991, sometimes called the "Perfect Storm," in which two weather systems combined with Hurricane Grace to wreak havoc at sea.

O is for Osprey

Ospreys near the water roost,
in nests atop the highest spruce.
Looking far with sharp eyes,
it spies a fish and down it dives.

The osprey, sometimes called the fish hawk, is the provincial bird of Nova Scotia. They return to the province in late March after spending the winter in the southern United States, Central, and South America. They will return to their large nests, high above the ground, made of sticks and often bits of string, rope, plastic, and fabric gathered from careless human litter.

A favourite place for osprey to nest is on power poles, a dangerous habit that could kill the birds and cause power outages. To resolve this problem, Nova Scotia Power has been building alternative nesting sites for more than 20 years. These new nest sites look like power poles, but are safe for the birds.

Ospreys live on a diet of fish and can be seen flying high over bays and inlets. When the hawk sees a fish, it will hover in place until it senses the right moment. It dives down with wings folded and hits the water, then up it flies, most often with a fish grasped in its talons.

P p

P is for Peace

Cyrus Eaton showed the way
for peace throughout the world today,
a world that lives in harmony,
all nations living peacefully.

Cyrus Eaton was a scholar and philosopher. He grew up in the scenic village of Pugwash. As a young man he worked and put himself through McMaster University, becoming a millionaire by the age of 27. After losing his fortune in the Great Depression, he became even more successful with new ventures in mining and railroads.

In the 1950s he began hosting gatherings of intellectuals to discuss world affairs. This was during a time called the Cold War when nuclear weapons threatened the world. He offered his home in Pugwash, known as the Thinker's Lodge, for a conference in support of peaceful answers to world conflict.

The first Pugwash conference was held in 1957. Scientists from around the world gathered with nuclear physicist Joseph Rotblat to discuss alternative solutions to war. In 1995 Joseph Rotblat and the Pugwash Conferences on Science and World Affairs won the Nobel Peace Prize. The Pugwash Conferences continue today.

Created by sewing layers of material together, a quilt can be made from new fabric, or from scraps of used clothing. Quilting can be a fine art, or simply a way of making something practical. Rural women began making quilts as a way of socializing through quilting parties or "frolics." Working together, they could produce something useful and creative.

The Women's Institute of Nova Scotia, dedicated to improving the lives of rural women, helped develop quilt making through the exchange of skills, patterns, and competitions. Quilters could sell their quilts to help with the family income.

Quilting can be an act of generosity. Through the Women's Institute and the Red Cross, thousands of quilts were donated to people all over the world facing hardships such as fire, flood, war, and poverty. Today this generosity continues with the Mayflower Quilters' Guild.

Q is for Quilt

Quilts of many colours
made from clothes of times gone by.
With love they're stitched together,
to tell stories of our lives.

R is for Duck Tolling Retriever

Splashing, swimming with webbed paws,
through ocean surf or in a lake.
Tollers bring back ducks or sticks,
then give themselves a furry shake!

Rr

The Nova Scotia Duck Tolling Retriever, also called the Little River Duck Dog or the Yarmouth Toller, is the provincial dog of Nova Scotia. Originally bred as a bird dog near Yarmouth, Nova Scotia, in the early 1900s, they resemble the larger Golden Retriever.

Wild foxes have been known to catch ducks by taking advantage of their curiosity. The Toller, with its fox-coloured coat, uses playful antics, just as a fox does, to lure (toll) curious birds into range along the shoreline. Then, if the hunter is successful, the dog will bring the bird back to the hunter.

Most likely bred from the now-extinct Red Decoy Dogs of Great Britain, tolling and retrieving are both natural to the breed, and the Toller will almost end-lessly return with a tossed object. With a thick water-repellent coat, the Toller is well insulated from its native icy waters.

Intelligent and gentle with children, they are a popular family pet ... but make sure this lively dog gets plenty of exercise!

S is for Sable Island

Sable Island's dunes rise up.
Mother seals nurse their pups.
Horses run through shoreline waves,
where fog can last for days and days.

Sable Island is a sandbar located in the Atlantic Ocean, 160 km off the shore of Canso, Nova Scotia. It is often blanketed in dense fog. The island is centred between three major ocean currents—the Gulf Stream, the Labrador Current, and the Belle Isle Current. It has been the site of more than 350 shipwrecks.

Sable Island is a landscape of freshwater ponds, 30-metre-high dunes, fields of wild roses, and beach grass. It is the sole nesting grounds for the Ipswich Sparrow. Storm systems bring rare visitors to the island, such as migrating birds blown off course, and even the occasional bat. It is a favourite breeding ground for grey and harbour seals. Thousands of pups are born here each year. The island is perhaps best known for its wild horses. They are descendants of horses brought to the island to graze in the late 1700s.

The Sable Island Station is a crucial facility for many important research projects, including the study of weather and atmosphere. Because it is protected, anyone wishing to visit the island must obtain permission from the Canadian Coast Guard.

Ss

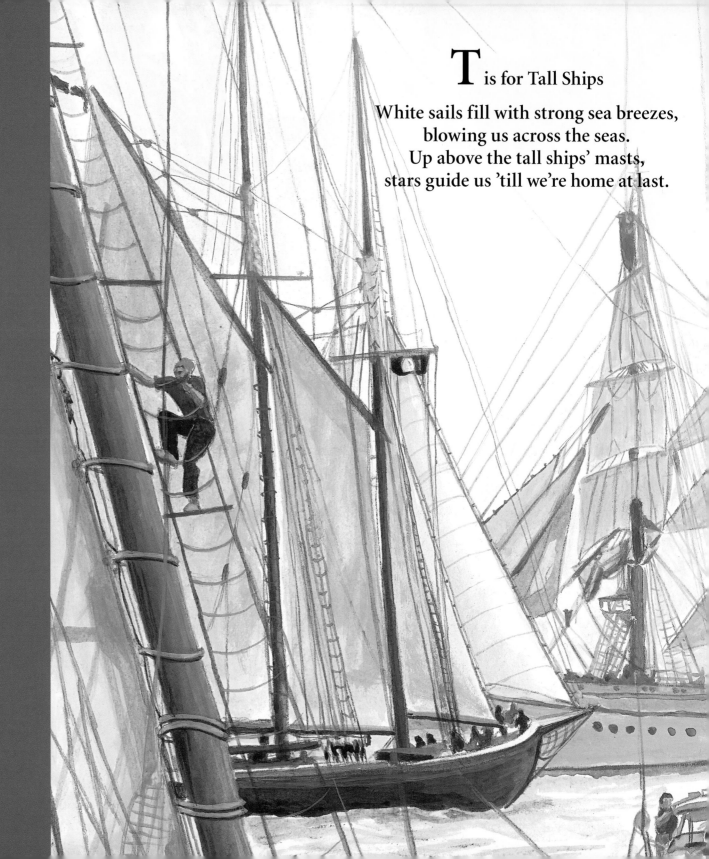

Tt

For centuries wind propelled ships across the seas on voyages of trade and discovery. Sailing ships were the primary means for ocean travel until the mid-1800s. When the steam engine was invented, ships no longer relied on wind power. Today sailing is a popular hobby. "Tall ship" is a modern classification applied to traditionally rigged sailing ships, such as topsail schooners.

The world famous Grand Banks schooner, the *Bluenose*, was designed by William James Roué. Built in Lunenburg and launched on March 26, 1921, her captain was Angus Walters. After a season fishing the Grand Banks, the *Bluenose* won the spot for the Canadian entry in the 1921 International Fishermen's Series, a race created for working ships. The *Bluenose* won four of the International Fishermen's Trophies, representing Canada at the Chicago World's Fair, and the Silver Jubilee of King George V.

Since 1937 the *Bluenose* has been on the Canadian dime. Today the *Bluenose II*, replica of the original, continues in the tradition as Nova Scotia's Sailing Ambassador.

T is for Tall Ships

White sails fill with strong sea breezes,
blowing us across the seas.
Up above the tall ships' masts,
stars guide us 'till we're home at last.

"Canaan Land" was a code used by travellers on the Underground Railroad when referring to Canada. During a time when slavery was legal in some parts of the United States, Canada became the hoped-for destination of African-Americans escaping toward freedom.

The lives of slaves were unbearably cruel, with physical hardship, impossible workloads, and the threat of being "sold away" never to see their families again. Even with a difficult life, it took great courage to escape into the night and travel, often on foot, the huge distances to the Canadian border. Over time, a system of safe houses throughout the United States, coded language and songs, and the pull of the North Star, became the Underground Railroad. The lives of all of those involved depended on silence. Once in Nova Scotia, many of these new immigrants travelled to the Quaker community in Dartmouth and to the Black communities of Nova Scotia, including Preston.

U u

U is for Underground Railroad

I am bound for Canaan Land,
on my journey going far.
I am bound for Canaan Land,
following the bright North Star.

V is for Veterans

Through April snow and big guns' roar,
  they fought their way uphill,
    and won that day in the Great War,
    our freedom treasured still.

Near the outbreak of World War I when the call went out for young men to serve overseas, over 3,500 Nova Scotians volunteered. In October 1916, Nova Scotia's Highland Brigade, which included the 85th Battalion, sailed for England. On April 9th, 1917 this group of soldiers was called into battle at Vimy Ridge, France.

From April 9th to April 12th, these troops, along with other Canadian soldiers, advanced under continuous enemy fire. Brave and well trained, their battle was hard fought and is considered by many to be the greatest victory for Canada in World War I.

During the remainder of the war, the 85th Battalion became known as the "Never-fails" for their courage and success in battle, winning 14 battle honours. Today we remember these brave soldiers, our veterans, who sacrificed and fought for the peace and freedom we enjoy today.

W is for Waves

When storms pound Nova Scotia's coast,
and nor'east winds do blow,
daring surfers catch a wave,
and put on quite a show.

Excellent surfing can be found year round in Nova Scotia, with some of the best wave action found in winter. Protected from head to toe, hardy surfers cannot resist the giant waves brought to shore by nor'easters.

The size of the waves increases with wind strength, the amount of time the wind has been blowing, and the distance the wind has travelled (fetch). Rogue waves, which can reach a height of 30 metres or more, are generally out to sea and are usually caused by the high winds of raging storms. Rolling waves are often found in protected beaches.

On the morning of December 6, 1917, Halifax was a bustling port. Canada was at war. The Mont Blanc, an ammunition ship loaded with explosives, headed into the harbour. The Imo, a Belgian ship, steamed into the narrows around the same time. Mixed signals caused the two ships to collide, causing a fire within the Mont-Blanc's hull. As the fire grew, crowds formed to watch. The Mont-Blanc had come to rest against Pier 6. Firefighters rushed to the scene as the pier began to burn.

With an explosion heard as far away as Cape Breton, Halifax was in ruins. More than 1600 people were killed from the explosion and the resulting surge of a tidal wave. Thousands were without shelter. Massachusetts, through the port of Boston, quickly sent aid to Halifax. Every year Halifax still sends a Christmas tree to the city of Boston as a thank you for their help.

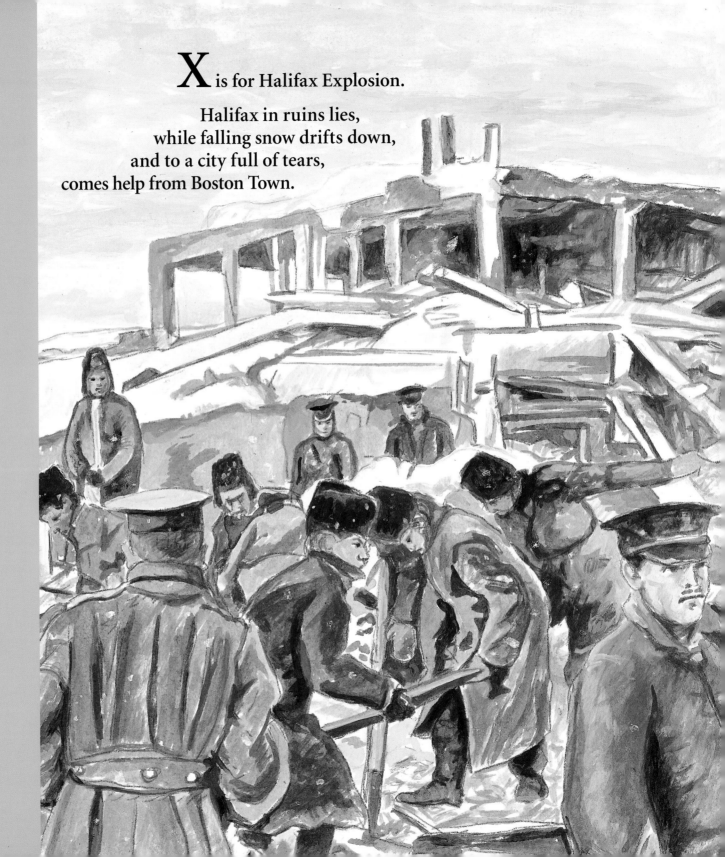

X is for Halifax Explosion.

Halifax in ruins lies,
while falling snow drifts down,
and to a city full of tears,
comes help from Boston Town.

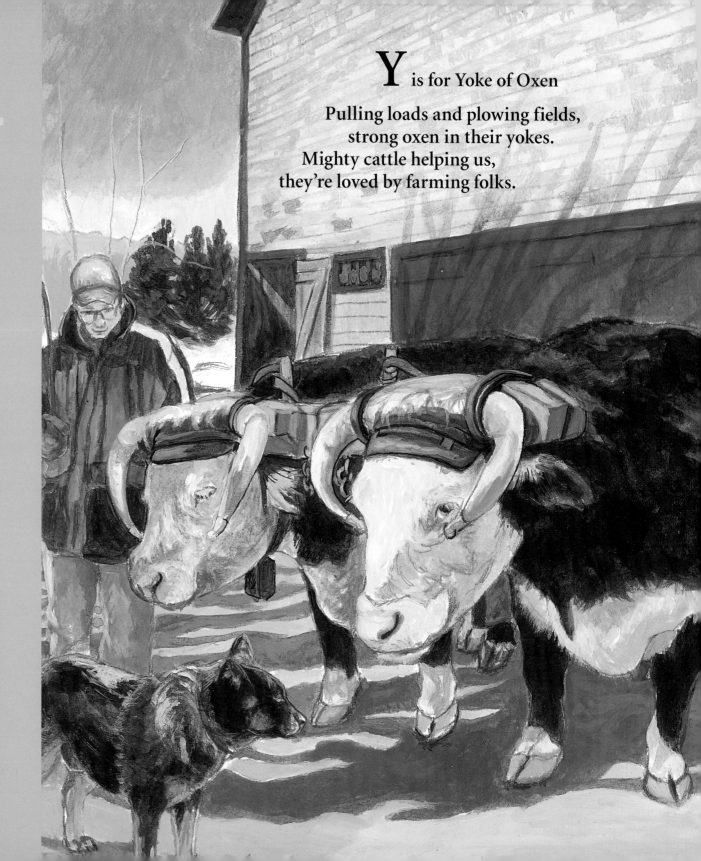

Y is for Yoke of Oxen

Pulling loads and plowing fields,
strong oxen in their yokes.
Mighty cattle helping us,
they're loved by farming folks.

Oxen came with Europeans to North America. From the early days of settlement, the ox was a favourite work animal on the Nova Scotian farm. Oxen needed much less care than horses, ate less grain, and were even-tempered and dependable. Though they moved at a slow pace, the oxen teams were very strong and helped farmers haul rocks to clear land, and to plow the fields.

The oxen were often hitched up into teams using a yoke. The yokes were made to fit over the necks, or the heads and horns of the oxen. Often these yokes were highly decorated, with bright paint, head pads, and tassels. They wore bells that could be heard for great distances so that farmers leading the oxen knew who was coming along the narrow roads, and they could find a spot where the two teams could pass easily. The command "Gee!" means turn right, "Haw!" means turn left, and "Get up!" means go forward.

Today oxen can still be found on small, rural farms, and featured in fairs and parades.

Zoology is the study of animal life. A fascinating place to study strange and amazing animal life is the Gully, a giant canyon in the ocean floor. The Gully is near Sable Island and has been named a Marine Protected Area by Fisheries and Oceans Canada.

At great depths the water pressure is crushing for creatures not adapted to it. Almost no light filters down from the surface. It is consistently cold at just a few degrees above zero. In this deep-sea world, strange creatures hunt their prey.

The viperfish is frightening in appearance, with a long snake-like body and jutting jaw, its teeth like miniature swords. It feeds on smaller fish, like the glacier lanternfish. Lanternfish have special light organs (photophores) that glow in this world of almost complete darkness.

The northern bottlenose whales are 6–9 metres long and can be found in the Gully all year. They dive deep and feed off plankton and squid near the canyon floor and can stay under water for an hour or more.

Zz

Z is for Zoology

Deep within the Gully's walls
a pod of whales dives down
into a world that is so deep,
there is no light around.

From Harbours to Highlands: More Nova Scotia Facts to Explore

1. What fruit is the Annapolis valley famous for?

2. Nova Scotia is the Latin word for what?

3. Where is the Cabot Trail located?

4. What structures were built in the settlement of Port-Royal to block the tides from the land?

5. Name two fortresses found in Nova Scotia.

6. What is the largest port in Atlantic Canada?

7. Where did Alexander Graham Bell fly his kites?

8. What are the largest turtles in the world?

9. What is the provincial bird of Nova Scotia?

10. Name some of the wildlife that can be found on Sable Island.

11. What ship can be found on the Canadian dime?

12. Which American city came to the aid of Halifax after the explosion in 1917?

13. Oxen are hitched up into teams using what device?

14. Name one species of whale that can be found in the Gully.

15. What tides are the highest in the world?

16. How long can the American Eel live?

17. What is Cyrus Eaton famous for?

18. Duck Tolling Retrievers are insulated from icy waters because of what?

19. Who were the "Neverfails"?

20. What season in Nova Scotia has the best waves for surfing?

21. One of the Seven Wonders of Canada is _____?

22. What are fossils?

23. How are quilts made?

24. Which lighthouse is the most famous in Canada?

Answers

1. Apples
2. New Scotland
3. Cape Breton Island
4. Acadian Dykes
5. The Citadel and The Fortress of Louisbourg
6. Halifax Harbour
7. Baddeck
8. Leatherbacks
9. The osprey/fish hawk
10. Sparrows, seals, wild horses
11. Bluenose
12. Boston, Massachusetts
13. Yoke

14. Northern Bottlenose
15. Bay of Fundy tides
16. Fifty years
17. Pugwash Conferences
18. Their thick, water-repellent fur coats
19. The veterans who fought in the 85th Battalion in World War I
20. Winter
21. Pier 21
22. Preserved remains of animals and plants embedded in rock
23. By sewing layers of material together
24. The Peggy's Point Lighthouse

Susan Tooke

Susan Tooke is an award-winning artist whose repertoire includes painted murals, landscapes, portraits, and digital imaging montages. She has exhibited her artwork across North America. Susan has illustrated several picture books, including *F is for Fiddlehead: A New Brunswick Alphabet*, also by Sleeping Bear Press. *B is for Bluenose* is the first children's book she has both illustrated and authored. Susan lives in Halifax, Nova Scotia, with her family.